When The Mask Slips

Narcissism Does Not Discriminate...

by Simply Sharon

Dorrance Publishing Co
585 Alpha Drive
Suite 103
Pittsburgh, PA 15238
Visit our website at *www.dorrancebookstore.com*

ISBN: 979-8-88812-377-5
eISBN: 979-8-88812-877-0

Narcissism does not discriminate...

Man, woman, gay, straight, transsexual, bisexual or nonbinary, it crosses all genders. They can be Black, White, Tan, Green, Purple, any color or races. They can come in any form mother, father, husband, wife, lover, best friend, coworker, boss, uncle, aunt, cousin, and even children. Anyone, anywhere, in any kind of relationship from any religious background to atheist, basically any human on the planet.

It also crosses all monetary class: rich and poor and everything in the middle. It doesn't matter how smart or mentally challenged you are, if you have gotten your doctorate or worked your whole life. From Ivy League educations to life on the streets, at one time or another you have been victim to a narcissist or you would not be reading this book.

In case no one told you today, you are worthwhile and valuable. This world needs your shine. There is only one you! I have helpful hints inside this book if you are still struggling. If you have healed, I am proud of you! Take a bow. This by far is the hardest thing you ever had to do, but look how much you have gained.

Welcome all, you are accepted here.

This book is dedicated to all the narcissists in my life that taught me my value and worth, who taught me the sun will come up without you to command it and life without you is always better than life with you (no matter what you claim). Thank you for teaching me all my survival skills and having faith in Myself as

The POWER of ONE!

Thank you, Lord, the Most High, the Devine, The Alpha, the Omega, and the Omnipresent Who never once left his Earth Angel!

*Thank you to the one person in this world who **always** believed in me.*

Who left too soon to read my book, My loving sister. I did it, Trishie!

I sit here surrounded by silence
There's nothing more I can do
You left me with nothing but questions
Just heartache and deceit from you

You took your paintbrush and created
A world that was beauty to see
Of all the love that we wanted
but it was only illusion for me

I noticed that you were changing
The distance between us was vast
I didn't realize the world you were living
Had a vicious and jealous new cast

You swim in the tide of illusion
a different mask for wherever you are
Peppered with a sexual addiction
for young girls you pay at the bar

The narcissist picks out the players
Carefully selecting his prey
They listen to his creation
Mesmerized with nothing to say

Everything you told them you wanted
All the plans you had for your life
Then they told you together we can get it
if you would love me and be my wife

Until you notice something changing
It starts small with them adding some space
And then not liking your friends and family
All your memories they start to erase.

All that they promised starts dimming
So the harder and harder you try
To keep the illusion from ending
But then you start to receive alibis

The silence they dealt you is deafening
The cruelty more than one soul can take
They work you until you are frantic
with lies that they try to fake

When you start to see the mask falling
and specter that lies underneath
It's almost an unrecognizable version
Of the person that they claimed to be

When you confront them as to why is this happening?
They tell you "it's all in your head"
But the horrible games that they're playing
Makes you think that you're better off dead

I feel sorry that that they are so wounded
So hurt from some childhood pain
You can't understand why they hurt you
But I suppose they need someone to blame

They settle for anyway to hurt you
Bring you into their world of lack
The only thing that can save you
Is running and turning your back

Their concept of love is controlling
Punishment and fear
But they're really full of self-loathing
No matter how they make it appear.

It's hard to pick up the pieces
Because some of them they do hide
But one day it will all cease to matter
When you're leaving them turns the tide

But every so often it happens
That the narc loses his way
That their new source of enjoyment isn't better
So they spy on what you're doing today

WHEN THE MASK SLIPS

There comes a day when they think they miss you
If they can even muster the feeling
To come back again with a new painted tale
So you'll lay there and look at the ceiling

No one can tell you to leave them
You have to decide when you are done
Of the lies and deceit and mistreatment
Your life's nothing like it had begun.

You walk out into the universe
Not knowing where it will lead
With your heart so badly broken
You're not even sure it will bleed

But each day turns into another
Now a year has surely gone by
They leave you with nothing but questions
The biggest will always be WHY?

Chapter One
First things first...

First, let me start by telling you **THIS IS NOT YOUR FAULT**. In fact, if you have been targeted by a narcissist you should consider yourself a very decent human being. To appeal to a narcissist you must first be kind and loving and self-sacrificing. You want to please and be liked and accepted. You're generous and giving of yourself and you love freely without reservation. You are empathetic and compassionate. You may be a little naive and/or a little too trusting but, all-in-all, a nice person to know and love.

Didn't we all believe this was exactly what we should be?

Weren't we taught to be kind to your friends or you won't have any. Respect authority in all its forms teachers, elders, policeman, coaches, priests, and nuns. Be honest at all cost. Don't lie, cheat, or steal. That was my life in the '60s as a child.

What we should have been taught was respect should be earned not given; you should respect people who respect you. Reason out who to listen to instead of blatantly following and who to question. Not everyone in authority has your best interest at heart. Be careful with yourself, not all people are good. We should have been given a list of people you can trust hands down, and then question the rest. Be good to yourself and keep yourself safe. Taking care of you is not selfish but necessary.

Authority gives power and is a great tool unless the person wielding it uses it unjustly. Power should never be used to manipulate nor control where it is not needed. One of the greatest tools of the narcissist is the power to manipulate any given situation and control those around them. You know those times when you are completely in the right and justified in your feelings, but after an hour of speaking with them, they can manipulate and twist things in such a way that not only are you so confused where the point actually went but they have you questioning yourself if you were wrong in the first place. They perfect the art of manipulation with such mastery that they leave you feeling confused about your **own** thoughts. It's the confusion that keeps you stuck and unable to direct a successful outcome to any conversation or chain of events.

I once heard someone say that "twenty different people could witness a car accident and their renditions would be close but ultimately each person would have a slight difference in what they actually saw." But if a narcissist were to enter the room and speak with them, when the people were asked again, they would all have the same story, but it would not be their story, it would reflect what the narcissist said and nothing else.

You are not stupid, gullible, or irrational; they are just very good at what they do! You are not overly sensitive because you have the ability to feel, something completely foreign to a narc. They lost that ability a long time ago.

Their power lies in their charm, their mesmerizing eyes, and your need to be liked by them. Why not? They are charismatic, cunning, self-assured (so they appear) and well liked by those around them. They all carry some sort of what I call "a presence." They stand out in a crowd, like a beautiful eagle soaring through the sky, majestic and regal until it swings down and grasps in their talons an unsuspecting less-skilled opponent who is literally no match for them and squeezes the life right out of them.

A little dramatic you might think, but if you are a survivor of their viciousness you have a slight grin on your face and are nodding your head in agreement. This is a no-nonsense survival guide from experience not a PhD, so if you are looking for fancy words and theories, this is not the place.

Chapter Two
The Truth is...

Repeat after me, <u>**Not everyone is going to like you—with or without reason. Period!**</u> There, does that feel better to get it off your chest? Release the notion that you can go to school or work or anyplace and if you're good enough and kind enough everyone will like you. They won't. No matter how hard you try there are people in this world who want nothing more than to dull your shine. They have a multitude of reasons for doing so, mostly the energies of jealousy or envy. Energies are embodied by anyone, as I said earlier, completely nondiscriminatory. When I talk about these energies, you will see how they will be embodied in different people in your life. They are not all narcissists.

Every one possess narcissistic qualities, just like we all have the ability to choose evil over good, questionable decisions over solid ones, and risk-taking behaviors even when we know better. All of us are guilty of this on one occasion or another, which in of itself does not make us a narcissist.

The narcissist seeks to destroy that which he envies even to his own determent. He plays the perfect victim to the scenario he creates. If they take part in risk-taking behavior and get caught, which is rare because they are fabulous liars, but on the off chance they do get caught, it will never be their fault, EVER!

They take no accountability for any of their actions, and by doing so, nothing and I do mean nothing is ever their fault or responsibility. It was who they were with, where they were at, and the social pressures involved. Never, will it be their fault for making the decision to partake. That way they will never ever have to apologize unless a meaningless halfhearted apology is what you're after to stay in whatever relationship you are in with them. Then they will just say "It will never happen again." What they really mean is: "It will never happen again till next time"—never really facing accountability for their actions.

The majority of us are perfectly capable of looking at a situation and discerning what part of this was actually our fault. Maybe not all of it but there comes a point when your actions were the catalyst for what went wrong. In dissecting the situation to see what part is your own culpability, we respond with the appropriate apology. Even if, after looking at the situation, maybe we don't see the other person's point of view clearly, the sheer fact we hurt our person enables us to apologize for the act of hurting their feelings or wounding them in some way, thereby acknowledging their feelings as valid.

Accountability does not exist in the narcissistic train of thought. It will forever be something or someone else's fault. Therefore, how could you possibly expect an apology for anything that was not their fault. To take this to another level—how could you possibly even think to accuse them of anything? This will lead them to attack your character, which was never in question in the first place. It will be forever your neediness, your need to control, your lack of trust, your accusatory nature, and you're making something out of nothing, which is a direct reflection of their own selves projected onto you to confuse and avoid. In a loud, finger-pointing, way, which leaves you scratching your head about how you got here. Remember, they are incapable of truly loving/liking anyone because they detest themselves.

Remember, it's not you…it's them.

Chapter Three
Little by Little they belittle...

Another tool a narcissists uses is **breaking your confidence in yourself**. If you have no confidence, they keep you stuck and trying harder to please the unpleasable. It's a vicious, mean thing to work on stripping someone of their confidence and self-worth.

To them, though, if you don't realize your self-worth and lack the confidence to tell them to get lost, then in turn they win and you stay stuck. Who else would want you? You're not worthy of love. You're not thin enough or too thin. You're not tall enough or too tall. You're not smart enough or too smart. You work too much or not enough. You're too loud or too quiet. They are always putting you in endless competition with others to show you clearly how you lack in every direction.

It's a non-winnable game of mental abuse so you run yourself ragged trying to be whatever it is this week your person has decided you need to be in order to reach an unattainable goal—your person to be happy to be with you. Then without you realizing it, day-by-day, month after grueling month, you begin to realize you will never be tall enough, smart enough, sexy enough or good enough to please your person.

You contemplate leaving because the hurt in your soul is so bad you can't take it anymore, but then their words begin to replace reality. Maybe I am not good enough, what if I can't make it on your own, and what if everyone will believe the lies said about me once I'm gone. Your person's little bites begin to take hold. The seeds of doubt begin to grow into a forest to blind your way. Maybe if the house was cleaner and grass was shorter and your person's favorite meal was waiting when they got home. Maybe then you would be worthy.

You would be worthy for whom, exactly? Some self-loathing bully to show you some of their attention and fake adoration they poured all over it. Just to have good day, when he pretends to be exactly what he was at the beginning that sold you into this fantasy in the first place. How long has it been since you've seen a glimpse of the person you first met or better yet a glimpse of who you were before you met them? When you weren't so full of anxiety trying to keep up the ever-increasing demands placed upon you. When was the last time you had a day to yourself to do anything you want without worrying about what he was up to or being texted 800 times because they live in the land of extremes?

No one likes traffic but to someone involved with a narcissists traffic can create the beginning of a question and answer session to rival the French inquisition. You get accused of doing something when doing nothing all of the time because "Evil sees as Evil does." They project onto you what they are doing when they are late so you are naturally guilty of doing the same things. When in reality you truly were just stuck in traffic. They degrade and belittle as a way of gaining control because this is truly to them all a game to win at all costs.

What they don't realize is it is a game no one wins because in the process of trying to destroy you, they destroy the very relationship they sought in the first place. But for them it's on to the next source that they can use and manipulate. You, though, are left wondering why and how someone could be so mean and cruel. You are the one left licking the wounds afraid to trust anyone. Don't! Be the phoenix that rises from the ashes stronger and wiser than ever before. Above all things, don't let them beat you. If you don't heal and remain broken, every relationship going forward will end in a disaster. Don't carry the relationship with the narc into the next. It is not the new person's fault either. That is why healing is so important.

Solve the issues of your mother or father if they were your narc. Do not pass those horrible beliefs on to your children. Take what they taught as examples of what you never want to be. Learn from abuse; do not continue it. Stop these cycles by healing YOU.

Chapter Four
The Mask Slips...for the first time

It's almost unfathomable to all of us survivors looking back on what started out as the most perfect relationship has ended up in this sick twisted play of confusion, turmoil, and chaos. There were warnings we all chose to ignore. Out of character behavior that came out of nowhere unprovoked. Everyone can have a bad day, but as extreme as it was, it should have been cause for concern. Then the little lies, the disappearing and the need for constant control over you.

All of us can remember the day when the illusion comes crashing down and you see the mask slip for the first time. Usually the first breakup. The first time when you have taken all you can and the monster immerges. When the narcissist feels threaten. When fear comes to him that you have figured it out or close to it. The outburst of outbursts, a fight like no other happens, words that make a sailor cringe and threatening behavior and you're not sure if this will be it or not. You run, fight or flight, there is only one choice. The tears and fears merge as one; you can't think; you can barely make sense of what you are doing.

Who was that? Surely this cannot be the person you have tried to please, that you have bent over backwards for, and invested in the future with. The lines in the road blur like the thoughts in your head,

No matter how you dissect it—and believe me, you do over and over, all night crying in disbelief. The pain hurts like no other. No matter how hard you try to make sense of it, you can't because this part of the play is illwritten on your behalf. This is the narcissist's part. They have played this part over and over in many relationships. This is the part where they decide if you're worth it or not. If you will still want to be a member of their supporting cast or if you know too much to bother when there is so much supply out there for them.

If you were a good source of supply to the narcissist, they will come back with all that they had in the beginning that worked so well on you but to the power of ten. My friend, this is better known as the love-bombing stage.

Love bombing, appropriately named *love* because that is what we all want to stop the pain but *bombing* to keep it in perspective. They fix the mask and slip back into the illusion, they beg you to come back, say that it will never happen again, that it wasn't them. They were just out of it with the thought of you leaving. They can't live without you.

They need you to come back and take care of their world of lack. After all "if you weren't doing this or saying that it wouldn't have happened" says the narc. Remember the bottom line: it will never be their fault. Your actions were surely the catalyst for any altercation. Not their horrible behavior and disrespect. They will never understand the meaning of the word respect as they do not respect their own selves. They just focus on filling their desires and self-satisfaction with as much forethought as a five-year-old—act first, take risks, and think later because the self-satisfaction comes in the moment and the moment only.

Unless they are plotting, then they take the time to work on the perfect setup. It's a cycle that goes on and on. The only way to make it stop is to jump off the carousel, but the speed at which the changes take place makes it a risky act. Be brave, stop the cycle, jump now for dear life and block, block, block.

No amount of love will change them, truly they are incapable. By the time you meet the narcissists, they are damaged beyond repair. That in and of itself is sad but does not diminish their ability to inflict pain and torture to everyone around them.

This probably won't happen to you the first time, unfortunately because kind, decent, loving people will want to "save them from themselves." We see "glimmers of hope" and feel "guilty on giving up on someone you love." That is the very thing they count on: your need to help to make them "better," so this story will continue on, no one can tell you to leave. Well, they can and do, but it will fall on deaf ears until you are ready. Think how many people you have spoken to while a wreck in an ocean of tears. They say you have to leave, that this is awful for you, but somehow we manage to make excuses for them so "they don't look so bad." When you hear yourself making excuses, listen to them. You're making up stories to cover up the fact the person you love is mean and hurtful. They don't deserve your time or your love. They will just suck your life force right from you. If you think it doesn't show, think again. Soon you've gained weight from all the stress and your emotions are taking a hit, leaving your face tattered and worn. You can't sleep because your thoughts are keeping you awake.

"Look at you, who will want you?" they say. "Listen to yourself, you sound crazy." Why? Because the truth you're speaking is getting too close, so to throw you offtrack you're needy, overly sensitive, and clingy. They destroy your self-esteem as a means to an end. Then, when they go missing and return, you should be happy they came home at all.

Deep down inside they envy your strength and push you to see how much you can take. They are mesmerized by how this thing called "Love" you cry about enables them to treat you however they want. Those feelings are so warped or removed completely from them to such a degree, you're like a science experiment to them, watching as they learn your triggers, where your insecurities lie so they can use them against you.

Winning is all that matters, at all cost.

Chapter Five
All is well or is it?

Being in the **love-bombing** phase can be almost euphoric as you haven't been in your full-blown illusion for a long while. However, you're not the same person as you were at the beginning. You have mastered a few things; you are not as trusting as before. Although you can't put your finger on it, you feel something is amiss in this illusion that wasn't there before. You want it so bad to be real that you turn your head on the warnings and delve right into it full throttle trying to please, eager to start anew.

You believe the "I'm sorry" because you have never heard it before. Your mind wants to believe what your heart is screaming, but on some level you know it's not the same. You're inner voice is telling you, keep your guard up. All your emotions are in total conflict. Your soul is not at rest, there is no peace here.

You walk around on egg shells not wanting to create a stir. You feel whatever was there is slipping away or changed forever. The same routine starts surfacing like trying to swim against the tide, you feel yourself drowning as the disapprovals return and your sense of self-worth starts falling like the temperature on a cold November day. There's nothing you can do. The constant picking on you has returned along with the self-righteous attitude.

Nothing you do is right, everyone everywhere is better than you. The love-bombing was just that, getting you back just to set you up for destruction. *What now?* you think. Everyone thought you foolish to go back and now you have to tell them you were wrong. After all your justification and defending your narc, you returned only to let it all happen again. The depth of sorry is hard to swallow. You start to believe it is your fault, that you are stupid, who would return to have it happen again? Let me tell right now, millions of people do.

You are not stupid and you are not alone. You love this person in all the imperfection, but at what cost? That's the real question. What are you getting out of this except a one-way trip down insanity lane. Where did all the happiness go?

The darkness is engulfing you. How can you stop it? Where can you turn? You don't have enough money, you fear no one will believe or want to help you because you will go through all this drama only to return. They have watched it with their own eyes. Unless you look deep inside yourself and stand in the mirror. What do you see? Are you happy? Are you tired of crying yet? You don't know what direction to go in because somewhere along the way you gave control over your own life to someone whose dragging it to hell. You were an actor in someone else's play. Recognizing is step number one. Deciding to figure out a way to escape it is number two.

Chapter Six
This is a game you cannot win. Period! Face the facts first.

There are no do-overs, no common ground they can understand, God forbid, no justice to this situation. The only way to save yourself is by getting out. If you try to treat fire with fire, you will be burned down in a half second. Narcs have spent their whole lives in this mixed up menagerie they call relationships. They perfected their skills long before you came along. Whatever broke the narc in the first place destroyed their ability to love on a conscious level.

MOVE IN SILENCE

Take down your social media, all of it. You will never be able to share, repair, or complete any thoughts with narc again. It doesn't matter why, when, or how it happened; you hit a breaking point of which you know there is no return if you are to survive. Change your phone number. Give it to only a few people closest to you. Probably with whom you are staying if you haven't socked away enough money to make it on your own yet. I'm going to release you from this—you are not a loser because you don't have enough money to set yourself up right because the narc had a hand in that too. You must find a way to go. Save yourself. If you can't find your way, pray! Doesn't matter to whom you pray, just a being of light and goodness, the Devine, Jehovah, the Universe, Buddha, or Jesus…whatever you believe that will help you. Pray for strength and guidance.

Only we have the keys to free ourselves; no one can do it for us.

All the "friends" will ask questions, they report back even the ones you expect the least. He sends them because he is busy not caring what you are doing.

They will stalk you on the internet, cover all your social media. Spread lies and rumors. Stalk your work, your home—always lock your car! This is how they make you question your sanity. People start to think you're crazy. You did the unforgivable: you left a narcissist. They do not want you happy. They want you destroyed. Doesn't that tell you something? They gossip and drag your name through the mud. Let me reassure you—when the dust settles, you will know exactly who your friends are and who they are not. No more guesswork. If they did not stand by you, guess what? They were never your people. Remove them, all of them and start fresh.

Remove if you can all connection to the narc. The peace of mind you will eventually feel will be well worth it. Where you can build the world you want to live. Like a painter with a fresh palette, all things are possible. The forestry department burns down sections of the forest when it's dying or thinning or sick. They know without the sick trees, a new lush forest will grow in its place. I never said this would be easy. It's heartbreaking as a matter of fact. We are all here to learn, sometimes through making mistakes. You will never know what strength you have until you have no other choice but to trust yourself enough to count on your own inner strength. That's when we grow. That's when the process of expanding comes. Like giving birth to a new life, you must go through the pain; there's no way around it, but you will emerge stronger, smarter, and wiser than ever before.

If someone doesn't want to be in your life or be for your greater good, then… LET THEM GO! Rejection is God's protection.

Chapter Seven
Where does the narcissist come from?

It's a sad story really that the majority of narcissists are born from childhood trauma or wounding. Somewhere along the way, through sexual abuse, neglect, lack of love, or just a severely dysfunctional household, these people develop. Their ideas of love and how to give and receive love becomes warped by the world they witnessed and lived in as a child. They see these situations and relationships through the eyes of child. Even though they are now adults, when something triggers them, the child, the inner soul's wounding resurfaces.

This is often when you find yourself thinking, are you kidding me? This makes no sense. The tantrums and acting out, the warped version of love, and the thought process, their need to control everything and everyone because as a child they had no control of their environment. Their desire to be liked, admired, and sought after is so compelling they will go to great lengths to achieve it, including and not limited to creating characters as swiftly changing as a chameleon to any given environment. They love to appear larger than life. They like to project themselves as the golden child where normal rules do not apply them. Unfortunately, this is all a façade and being such has a short life expectancy. It is extremely hard to continue for any length of time.

Inside however, they are sad, lonely, and empty unable or capable of loving themselves or others in a healthy manner. They possess little to no coping skills and at times reflect the attitude of a toddler. They saw you at the beginning as a shiny new toy. You were full of all they did not possess light, laughter, and love. You were probably liked by all who knew you and had a decent job and had your life together. Jealousy thy name is narcissist.

Attracted like a moth to a flame they study their prey like a circling vulture waiting to gain knowledge and understand their subject. That is why at the beginning, they listen to every word you say. You think to yourself "someone hears me, really hears me." Ahhh, but they listen attentively to use it against you and drag you into a tailored illusion just for you. They ask all the questions, if you remember correctly, adding very little of their own life to the conversations just enough to make you think they have a heart and appear vulnerable. While the whole time they are using the info to create the perfect illusion to trick you into believing.

They seek what they desire till you figure out what is going on behind the mask and running just beneath the surface. They appear to have it all together and for a while they pull it off as if an actor playing a role. But like all tragic love stories, this, too, will end when they are done with you and have used you all up.

That's when they discard you like yesterday's newspaper without a second thought. Then they are off to the next shiny new source to use and destroy. You are left wondering how someone who professed to love you could be so calculating and cruel. Completely void of emotion, it fazes them not. The pain from the realization of that is completely unbearable. You invested so much time, love, and tears into this person to be tossed aside like a nothing.

You, my dear broken heart, are not a nothing. They are. You feel, you cry, and you agonize, but you are alive. Emotions, no matter what kind, make you realize you are alive. You're not a robot unable to feel or a monster who sits back bewildered at someone's pain because their heart is breaking. They broke a long time ago and it fractured them in such a way they would never feel emotions of any kind again, unless it is desire and control but always without love.

Sex is the closest they come to feeling anything and even at that there is an element of fear, pain, and control. You did not cause what happened to this narcissist. Likewise you cannot fix it. Let me repeat this most important part:

YOU CANNOT FIX WHAT IS WRONG WITH A NARCISSIST.

The only one that can fix them is them if at all. The bad thing of it is, in their mind there is nothing wrong with them. They are entitled and above all rules. They play the victim in everything to keep from having accountability for what they have done and make the appearance of having feelings. They are so self-loathing for they lack all the emotion and feelings they see you have. Instead of consoling you, they hate you for it. They are completely incapable of empathy. This is why they reach out for empaths. Like a body builder reaching for the exact vitamin they lack, they reach for your light to feed on it and drain you of it.

Over the years I heard so many excuses why people stay in these no-win situations. From "vows before God" to "but He needs me" and let's not forget the favorite "you can't give up on someone you love." Love is a two-way street.

Letting someone abuse you in hopes that someday they will change is not helping anyone, especially you. Allowing this is enabling the narcissist to continue to do so. Enabling has a catch phrase connotation; here are similar phrases that aren't so catchy. Allowing someone to belittle you and your needs, empowering the narcissist, entitling them to continue without consequences, and making it possible for them to seek their sick gratification in devaluing you as a human being is a disservice to everyone involved, including you.

One person cannot give their all while the other person takes it all. One person cannot rule as dictator and the other person is enslaved in the relationship as if they dare say I cannot live like this. The narcissist, knowing full well they could never live under the same restraints imposed on you, states "Fine" and walks out, slamming a door behind them. The narcissist will toddler off to find some other unsuspecting soul who will be more than willing to do so for a while. Whose happy pictures will be posted on social media to punish and humiliate you. They will make you feel through text or email (if you don't block them) that there are others more willing and more capable of loving them than you.

Ultimately by doing so, they attempt to use this process to prove to you your shortcomings and unworthiness. Let me tell the reality of it all. If you have decided to walk away from the narc, then you are smarter than most and stronger than the ones that stay. The new supply they find will end up in the same way you are. As insane as this may sound, they use you and your relationship against the new supply in much the same way to get the new supply to surpass the goal of trying to be better than you. My old supply did this, that, and the other thing to make me happy; being with you makes me miss the old supply. There is also another undercurrent here. Not only does it keep the new supply trying harder and still feeling like she is surely sinking in quicksand, but they unlock the door for speculation of a departure to the old life. Indirectly making the new supply hate you so much you will never compare notes.

All the tracks are covered. Jealousy and envy are set into play with such vengeance while leaving you completely unaware of it even happening.

Chapter Eight
Reciprocity (noun) A situation where each enjoys an equal benefit

Let's examine the relationship you feel you can never leave. Above you will see the definition of reciprocity. What part of this relationship is equal? Is it the part where only the things important to the narcissist have priority? Is it the part where what's important to you is the least cause for concern? Where anything is more important than whatever your needs are?

Where are you in the relationship? Have you gotten to the point where it's useless to even ask about what you desire? That you ask yourself "do I even care enough about attending this event to go through what it will entail to bring it up?"

The longer you stay the worse it becomes until you're a ghost moving through your own life, that only the narc's needs are being met at all now and your identity is disappearing. What is it you wanted out of life again, I forget?

A narcissist has about as much reciprocity as a toddler in the "MINE" stage. It is truly remarkable how close to that toddler they have become, forcing you to attain the role of a bad mother who can't make parameters and to give in to his tantrums and selfishness for fear of losing them.

Picture, if you will, the sun with the planets revolving around it. This is the setting of the narcissist, the narc, of course, playing center of the universe, their universe in a galaxy few will ever travel to. Swirling around are the planets or players, if you must, in this universe, each with a role to provide. Notice they are all only a supporting cast to the narc. They love to be surrounded by yes people who are empty and needy and enjoy chaos. So if you think you are the only one, think again.

What is it that you brought into this so-called relationship? How much effort do you put into it? How much time is absorbed by the narc? Now reverse the roles. How much time does the narc put in? How far do they sacrifice for you? Are they there when you need them supporting you and helping you?

They have no concept of give and take…. It's continually take, take, take. When you bring this up to them, if you even dare, you're overexaggerating. When they hurt your feelings with these senseless games or emotional abuse, it's just you being oversensitive. Grow up! They say, which is hysterical sense they have no plans of ever acting like an adult or being rational or having any accountability All are forms of being an adult including a civil conversation where you are not under attack for standing up for yourself, where someone will actually listen without shaking their head as if you just escaped from an insane asylum. Normal adult conversations about relationships have resolutions. Nothing ever gets resolved with a narc because, to them, it's fine just the way it is, and why wouldn't it be? They have it made.

Never try engaging the narcissist on his level. The narc is too skilled to take on. You will lose; the only winning is to end the game. I can't stress that enough.

Chapter Nine
Future planning or planning an exit?

They have a wonderful way of projecting a future of everything you desire. They are smart and skilled at this horrible game. Yet, they have no intentions of ever making this future of theirs come true. It just bides them time to secure a new avenue till they can discard you and skip on to the next in case the pressure gets too much.

They will promise anything: marriage, a great vacation, a new home, and all with you in mind to share it. The only problem is they have already sold the same scenario time and time again. That's why it rings so true—practice.

You are not foolish to believe it; they are the Magician in Tarot at a low vibration, of course. They use all the tools at their disposal to lie, cheat, manipulate, and use you. Their stories go round and round till you're so confused you don't know which end is up.

"I thought you said in November we were going on a trip?"

"No, that's not what I said. I said I had a trip in November for work."

It doesn't matter which way you ask the questions, the answers will always be the same "You're confused; you don't listen to me when I talk." That statement is the complete opposite; you do listen to what they say that's why you are confused because the story is always ever-changing. You're not crazy; you are just getting close to discovering the narc is a born liar.

"I want you in my life; I want a future with us."

"I want to take care of you, buy a home, and put down roots."

Lovely right? Everything you wanted to hear, right?

"Next time, we go out I'll make sure to be with you and make you feel secure."

Always a future based on words only. They have no intention of making it happen, none whatsoever. They have sold this same notion to many others. It's just to get you to invest more into them with the hope that in the future, things will be better, more stable, and something to count on.

All their words are just another illusion to follow… a dream off in the distance to strive for and to keep you trying harder. While you're busy trying harder to make the illusion happen, they are weaving other tales to others. Pathological liars getting their means to an end and I do mean end. All the future promises are as delusional as the promises of the past that never held true.

They are on the low vibrational end of the magician, using all the tools they possess to trick, fool, and lie so they can use, abuse, and manipulate.

Chapter Ten
Silence is your greatest tool

The only way to escape the clutches of a narcissist is silence. Create space between you and your narc as best you can. Take time to breathe. Stop the anxiety of running around trying to do too much, love too much, and serve too much.

Take all of that energy and turn it inward. Try pleasing *you* for a change. Take the time you need to figure out where this all went wrong and pick up your pieces. Sit in a quiet space and try to stop all the noise they placed in your head.

You know why? Because you are good enough and you are worth it, regardless of what you have been told. You need to not answer the texts, the phone calls, and the emails. Ignore the others that come at you for them. If you have to take your social media down till you heal, do so!

Your soul needs you to be kind to it. Repair all the damage to your broken heart. Try to remember what life was like before and what it can look like after. I am not saying give up living; I am saying give up the illusion.

Start with silence. How long has it been since you could actually think about this relationship with a healthy mind. Remember laughing out loud and meaning it? If people ask, simply say I need this time for me. Self-care and healing is not selfish; at this point its survival. You've been wounded, deeply, although there are no open cuts to show the world. No one can truly understand the hold these people create with the mind torture they inflict unless they have been through it themselves.

I am here to say to you I have and from the depths of my soul I feel for each and every one going through this. There is a light at the end of this dark tunnel. I am proof. Unfortunately, you must do the work. You must remain strong even though you are shattered. Cry it out of your system. Go scream it into your pillow. Call them every name you know they deserve for what they have done.

Remember to draw strength from this. Take all of your hurt and pain and use it to build yourself even better than before.

Give your self-esteem a shot in the arm, go the gym, start eating a healthier diet, and change your hairstyle. Improve your mind and take a class. Write a book or journal even if it's just for you, but do not answer the phone. I did puzzles, read self-help books, went to church, prayed to the God and anyone that would help me, and cried for a year. I watched YouTube videos by the zillion all on narcissists. Every time I felt myself getting weak, I would put a show on and remind myself of just how horrible it all truly was. Little by little the pieces fell back into place.

One day I actually laughed and felt it!!! Imagine that, I didn't fake it. Then there was the day I didn't feel shaky for the entire day. I know to anyone who doesn't know, that sounds nuts, but if you have been where I was, you know exactly what that means.

When I emerged from what felt like a cocoon and broke free from all of that pain. The world was there. The one I remembered. Only this time I had new set of skills. I am no longer that naive person, but I am not tainted either because that would be letting the narc win. I centered myself and left all the people who had a hand in hurting me behind in the dirt where they belong.

I have no idea what the future holds, but I will be the one writing it. No one will ever take that power away from me again. If someone wants to be with me, we will walk hand in hand, side by side with mutual respect. I will say exactly how I feel at the sign of any red flag. Until you are strong enough, there is no need to address the narc in your life. In some cases, if you can do without ever speaking to them, great. Sometimes they are people like family who will be forever there. Just create good healthy boundaries around those relationships. Protect your heart and your soul. If not you, who will?

I hope that this book helps some people find a few answers or gives them a couple of ideas. If nothing else, that you come away knowing that at the very least you are not alone. There are millions of people who have suffered at the hands of a narcissist who has professed to love beyond measure. How possibly when they don't even love themselves and they are full of self-loathing.

Remember who sought after whom? Only to be told you are now not worthy. It's a game to them that they need to win at all costs.

What they fail to realize is they end up the biggest losers, full of regret of how they treated the people who love them. They can lie to everyone including themselves but at 2:00 in the morning, there is no one to lie to, the truth stares you right in the face. When you're old and not charismatic and good-looking as you used to be because that all fades. What then? They will be alone in a world of emptiness they created themselves, having lost the very people who cared about them.

We, though, the survivors of these self-absorbed envious people, we will heal and carry on. It might take us a few years to dust off the brutality of their hurt-filled games, but we will rise from the ashes. We will have lives filled with people who know our worth because the narcissist taught us when we stood up to them. We valued ourselves enough to walk away and end the game of which they will never win.

Reach inside, heal the hurt and take your life back. Free yourself from their control. If you can't do it on your own, get help. Do whatever it takes to save you. You are worth it!!! The world needs its empaths. I believe in you and the power inside you, one good person against the rest.

You will smile again and you will love again. When you do, it will be the best feeling because you mean it.

The only way to beat the narc is to not play the game. Good Luck, my friend, you got this!